Contents

PREFACE..1
CHAPTER ONE..2
INTRODUCTION 2
   TEAM 3
   OBJECTIVES OF TEAM 3
   TYPES OF TEAMS 4
   TEAM'S CONDUCTS AND MISCONDUCTS..6
   FACTORS CONTRIBUTING TO MISCONDUCTS IN A TEAM 7
   DEVELOPING A TEAM...8
      COGNITIVE..9
      AFFECTIVE 9
      PSYCHOMOTOR...10
CHAPTER TWO..11
   TEAMWORK...11
   CHARACTERISTICS OF TEAMWORK...12
   IMPORTANCE OF TEAMWORK 13
   BUILDING TEAMWORK...14
   BENEFITS OF TEAMWORK 15
   CHALLENGES OF TEAM/TEAMWORK...19
   HOW TO MAINTAIN TEAMWORK 21
   CONCLUSION 22

PREFACE

This book is designed bearing in mind the needs of organizations as regards to cooperation amongst the workers as a team to enable them reach their set goals.

The book is divided into two chapters. In chapter one we discussed in detail the concept of team, its objectives, types, conducts, factors leading to misconducts in a team and how to develop a team. In chapter two the author discussed the concept of teamwork, characteristics of teamwork, importance of teamwork, building teamwork, its benefits, challenges and how to maintain teamwork in a team.

CHAPTER ONE

INTRODUCTION

Just as it's one thing to join a team, but quite another to perform as a team member, no team can survive without teamwork. To make it simpler, it's one thing to create a team, but quite another to create a team that works. Teams can't last long without teamwork. Creating and maintaining a high performing team involves hard work and dedication. For any team to grow and maintain high standards, all the team members and the team leader must be ready to make sacrifices to ascertain the team's objectives. It involves all the steps for peaceful coexistence, elements of effective communication and a lot more.

TEAM

A team is a group of individuals (human or non-human) working together to achieve their goal.

As defined by Professor Leigh Thompson of the Kellogg School of Management, "team is a group of people who are interdependent with respect to information, resources, knowledge and skills and who seek to combine their efforts to achieve a common goal".

A group does not necessarily constitute a team. Teams normally have members with complementary skills and generate synergy through a coordinated effort which allows each member to maximize their strengths and minimize their weaknesses.

Naresh Jain (2009) claims that: Team members need to learn how to help one another, help other team members realize their true potential, and create an environment that allows everyone to go beyond their limitations.

A team is a group that has agreed to take on a specific task with the aim of achieving a common goal or objective. Team usually starts with a minimum of two people and it can grow to absorb more people or numbers depending on its type. Every organization, be it private or public is a team, and there could be sub-teams under a team. Creating teams under a team could be as a result of expansion or increase in productivity whereby the team would need subsidiaries to sustain high performance.

OBJECTIVES OF TEAM

A standard team should be guided by the stated objectives below:

- To share knowledge and ideas that will adequately enhance each member to play their roles in the development of the team.
- To give meaning and opportunities to a shared idea that will balance the physical, mental and emotional feelings of the members by giving them chances of trial and error.
- To provide opportunities for exceptionally gifted or talented members to develop at their own pace putting the interest of the team at number one priority.
- The team's vision should include the interest of the members as the top most target.
- To identify and provide solutions to existing community problems.
- To generate revenue that would contribute positively to the growth of the nation's local economy.
- To be there for each member at a time of need, be it celebration or grief.
- In some of the organizations that deal with sensitive information and security issues, there could be provision where members are allowed to share the status of their situations both at home and office and specify where the team can assist. This helps them to be mentally and emotionally balanced to be able to contribute positively to the team's growth.
- The team is home.

The objectives of a standard team are all the positive benefits that the members, community and the nation stands to gain as an added input towards national development.

TYPES OF TEAMS

These include but not limited to:

1. Formal: Formal teams are groups created under rules by Directors, Head of Resources or Managers and charged with carrying out specific tasks to help the organization achieve its goals. The HR Personnel and Managers are also two different bodies under the instructions of the Director. Example is that this type of team is always formed based on hierarchy, starting from Director then head of resources, then manager, then team leaders, then workers and staffs.

2. Informal: Informal teams are a group of individuals which are not officially set up by an organisation, they have no rules or guidelines and they work together to achieve a given purpose. Such groups develop within the formal organizational structure. This type of team usually meets during breaks, lunches or any other opportune times. They're usually people who share common interests, speak the same language and other personal relationships like fields of Studies.

3. Traditional: A traditional team is a group of individuals who work on interdependent tasks, who share responsibility for outcomes, and who work together at the same location. Examples of this type of team include, the task force, the conflict resolution and the quality improvement teams.

4. Self-directed: A self-directed team is a set of individuals in an organization who incorporate various talents and abilities to work toward a common goal or objective without the standard administrative oversight. This type of team only includes people who have built trust in each other.

5. Leadership: A leadership team is typically a group of owners, administrators and other staff members who make important governance decisions in an organization. It usually includes Chief Executive Officer (CEO's), Vice president, Chief Finance Officers (CFO's), Chief Operating Officers (COO's), and other upper level executives of the organization.

6. Problem solving: Problem Solving Teams are temporary structures that bring together leaders and team members from across the organization to focus on solving a specific problem. An organization may decide to dissolve or restructure this kind of team after the solution of a problem is found.

TEAM'S CONDUCTS AND MISCONDUCTS

Whenever people come from different backgrounds and agree to work to achieve a specific goal, there should be a blueprint that would serve as conduct to all the members of the team. Should such a blueprint be sabotaged which we term as misconduct, punishment would follow. Such conducts includes:

- Show respect to one another irrespective of age and ethnic groups. The eldest and the youngest in the team are equal. Different tribes, skin colors and mode of dressing should complement one another without any form of disrespect, though the team may have a dressing code depending on the kind of team.
- There should be no insult of any kind at the workplace or during the team meetings.
- Keeping to agreed time for any of the team events. Don't come behind schedule.
- Whatever happened in the team should remain within the team. Don't discuss your team outside unless for a good course and with permission.
- Don't take the team's property for use like personal property even if you're the team lead, it creates room for theft or envy.
- Don't always lead by command, as a team leader, you should rather lead by showing examples that your team members can emulate.
- The team should sympathize with any of her members who fall victim to any circumstances.
- There should be occasional capacity building for the team aimed at enlightening members and all team members must be in attendance.

All these are conducts that the team members are supposed to keep in mind and work with. Misconducts usually come in when the members or a member chose to disregard these guidelines.

FACTORS CONTRIBUTING TO MISCONDUCTS IN A TEAM

The following are some of the factors contributing to the misconducts in a team:
- **Lack of visionary leaders.** When the personnel who are acting as leaders or directors of a team or organization lack visionary skills or foresight, definitely the team will collapse because members would not have a clear picture of where they're headed.
- Insincerity factor. Lack of sincerity is one major factor that usually comes from both the members and team leaders. It often starts by keeping quiet when things go wrong or accepting an idea even when you don't agree with it.
- **Blaspheming;** lying to gain favour over your teammates from either the team leader or using the team's name to gain favour outside without the team's consent can also contribute to misconducts as everyone would feel they can do or say whatever they like.
- **Economic factor.** The team is supposed to bear some responsibilities for its members. But in a situation where the team lack financial strength to carry out some projects or workshops for its members and thereby making the members to contribute money in order to be trained in a particular field that is actually meant to benefit the team, then expect misconducts because each member would want a chance to practice their own personal idea even if such idea wouldn't benefits the team.
- **Lack of the right attitude to work.** Violation of Work ethics like absconding, coming late or leaving the workplace before closing time without a genuine reason or permission can create workload on other members and thereby stressing them up and reducing their productivity. It could also discourage those with the right attitude to work because everyone will start giving excuses for not coming to work or coming late or even

leaving the office before closing time. Proper punishment should be made available for whoever falls victim of this factor.

DEVELOPING A TEAM

The development of teams is always based on three levels- Cognitive, affective and psychomotor levels. We based our fact on Benjamin Bloom's taxonomy of education; Bloom's taxonomy is a set of three hierarchical models used for classification of educational learning objectives into levels of complexity and specificity. The three lists cover the learning objectives in cognitive, affective and psychomotor domains. These levels aren't meant only for education and learning, it can also be viewed in our daily lives and a proper organization can be formed following these levels step by step as we have discussed below.

COGNITIVE

By cognitive, I mean all the logical thinking as to how, what, when and why creating a team usually comes up during this level. Under this level we have team Development stage 1, forming:

Stage 1: Forming.

During the Forming stage of team development, team members are usually excited to be part of the team and eager about the work ahead. Members often have high positive expectations for the team experience. As a result of feelings, behaviour and the imaginary task ahead, lots of questions pop up. Questions like; how to fit into the team, the uncertainty they might encounter and how to perform well as a team.

AFFECTIVE

The Affective level shows the results that were obtained from logical thinking; how they were able to meet the expectation of each member and team's goal. Skills in the affective domain describe the way people react emotionally and their ability to feel other living things' pain or joy. Affective objectives typically target the awareness and growth in attitudes, emotion, and feelings. The stage 2, storming, comes in here.

Stage 2: Storming.

In this stage, as the team begins to move towards its goals, members discover that the team can't live up to all of their early excitement and expectations. Their focus may shift from the tasks at hand to feelings of frustration or anger with the team's progress or process. Members may express concerns about being unable to meet the team's goals. So, the storming stage would be how to fix the loopholes arising as a result of disagreements and anger. The team at this stage may decide to break their big dreams into small achievable goals to relieve its members of their frustration and make their goals an easy one.

PSYCHOMOTOR

Skills in the psychomotor domain describe the ability to physically manipulate a tool or instrument like a hand or a hammer. Psychomotor objectives usually focus on change and/or development in behavior and skills.

This involves all the team's efforts to facilitate struggles, both individually and collectively making sure that the team succeeds. Stage 3 and 4, Norming and Performing stages.

Stage 3: Norming.

During the Norming stage of team development, team members begin to resolve the discrepancy they felt between their individual expectations and the reality of the team's experience. The successful setting up of more flexible and inclusive norms would increase the sense of comfort and feeling of belonging among the members. There will be positive change in behaviour and willingness to share ideas or ask teammates for help. At this stage, all energy would be focused on how to achieve the team's goal.

Stage 4: Performing.

At this stage, the team's satisfactory progress can be seen from their collective ideas and performance. The team members now know each other's strengths and weaknesses and are ready to support each other by sharing productive ideas. This performing stage also gives room for division of labour amongst the team members based on their strength and capabilities. The commitment and competence of team members are already high.

Stage 5: Termination/Ending.

This isn't actually a part of team development, but in some cases, when restructuring happens, some teams do come to an end as a result of completion of their work or when there's changes in the organization's needs.

Sustaining performance.

How do you manage to stay on top as a high performing team? Just like in business, starting up isn't actually a big problem but how to stay on without falling. So it is with a team, what is the grace behind team's success, what really keeps a team going and recording more progress, do we just create a team and then it starts functioning, what exactly is capable of sustaining a team's performance. The answer is ' **teamwork**.'

CHAPTER TWO

TEAMWORK

Teamwork can be seen as the co-operation between those who are working on a task. This simply means when a group of people work together cohesively, towards a common goal, creating a positive working atmosphere, and supporting each other to combine individual strengths to enhance team performance.

Teamwork can also be defined as the ability to work together toward a common vision. It is the ability to direct individual accomplishment toward organizational objectives. It is the fuel that allows common people to attain uncommon results. (Andrew Carnegie)

It is the collaborative effort of a group to achieve a common goal or to complete a task in the most effective and efficient way.

Teamwork is the kind of work that teams are best configured to do. It is work that blends individual strengths so that they complement each other, and in doing so brings people together with a sense of familiarities and shared vision so that their strengths are applied in a common direction towards meaningful goals. It is called in French 'esprit de corps'.

CHARACTERISTICS OF TEAMWORK

After our explanations on the concept of team, its objectives, formation, types and teamwork, it is imperative to talk about the characteristics of teamwork. Despite the explanation of teamwork, there are still common characteristics of teamwork.

- Teamwork provides fast results. This is so because there is a distribution of labour based on skills and specialties. The highly intellectuals are allowed to share ideas that would enable them to walk through their targets with ease.

- The members demonstrate readiness to adapt to dynamic changes that occur as a result of environment, changes in the team's targets or even as a result of expansion.
- Majority of the team members are highly skilled. The sharing of ideas in the team gives the members an opportunity to learn different skills from each other as they work interdependently.
- Inquisitive members. Teamwork always comes with an inquisitive mindset as the members would always want to search and obtain any knowledge that will benefit the team.
- They have good abilities in logical thinking which exposes them to knowledge. This is so because all the team members have developed the feelings of belonging, so they are curious about what would bring development to the team.
- They maintain good relationships with their teammates and superiors both in and outside the workplace.
- Time management is very crucial to them. They will always keep to time because they wouldn't want to disappoint their team by bringing down its high reputation.
- Exercise of quality leadership style. Because there is a sense of belonging and good orientation about the team's conducts, there is maximum respect for the team captain and the captain in turn recognizes his teammates.
- There's always cooperation between the team.
- Focus is always on the team's goal and not individuals.

IMPORTANCE OF TEAMWORK

Below are some of the importance of teamwork:

1. Teamwork creates synergy – where the sum is greater than the parts. It deals in collective ideas and thereby limiting future errors.

2. It Supports a more empowered way of working, removing constraints which may prevent someone doing their job properly.

3. It encourages more leaner structures in the work environment, with less hierarchy.

4. It increases individual interests in the quest to attain the organizational goals and objectives.

5. It Fosters flexibility and responsiveness, especially the ability to respond to change without creating problems.

6. It Pleases customers. Customers who like working with good teams, sometimes may want to be part of the team having observed the kind of synergy that the team is growing on.

7. Promotes the sense of achievements. Whatever success the team recorded, would be for the team before the individual that made the team succeeded.

8. When managed properly, teamwork is a better way to work because it allows Interdependence whereby team members can lean on their colleagues to build their skills as it involves learning on the go.

9. It enhances organizational growth because of its collective nature of ideas.

10. It creates ties like family because there's this belief that an injury for one is an injury for all.

BUILDING TEAMWORK

To build teamwork in a team, there's a need for 'team spirit'. By team Spirit I mean the feelings of 'come what may, we stand as one.' And this involves the following points:

1. Avoid using languages understood only by few, adopt the use of universal language.

2. Identify and blend strengths of individuals so that they complement each other

3. Reform the people's sense of togetherness with a vision of where you are going

4. Align strengths with good teamwork in a common direction towards achievable goals.

5. Avoid favoritism as a team leader, but can reward a high performing skill to encourage others.

6. Be friendly as a leader and always wear a smiling face.

7. Be specific in your instructions to avoid confusion.

8. Give room to the members to explain their views and complement them on their struggles

9. Take your time to address a mistake in an appropriate manner without condemnations.

10. As a team lead, be open to your team members both within and outside the workplace.

BENEFITS OF TEAMWORK

1. Fosters Creativity and Learning

Creativity thrives when people work together on a team. Brainstorming ideas as a group prevents stale viewpoints that often come out of working solo. Combining unique perspectives from each team member creates more effective selling solutions.

Albert Bandura posits that people learn from one another, via observation, imitation, and modeling. What you have learned from your individual experiences is entirely different from your coworkers. Thus, teamwork also maximizes shared knowledge in the workplace and helps you learn new skills you can use for the rest of your career.

Collaborating on a project creates an enthusiasm for learning that solitary work usually lacks. Being able to share discoveries with the rest of your team excites employees and fosters both individual and team knowledge.

2. Blends Complementary Strengths

Working together allows the employees to build on the talents of their teammates. While your strength may be creative thinking, a co-worker might shine in organization and planning. Do not hesitate to share your abilities with the team.

Often, a team works well together because team members rely on each other to bring individual talents to the table. By observing the process behind these skills, you can learn how to combine your gifts and become a stronger team.

Every time you see your coworkers utilize a different approach in sales, you have a chance to adjust or improve your methods.

3. Builds Trust

Relying on other people builds trust, and teamwork establishes strong relationships with coworkers. Despite occasional disagreements, an effective team enjoys working together and shares a strong bond. When you put your trust in a coworker, you are establishing the foundation of a relationship that can endure minor conflicts.

Trusting your teammates also provides a feeling of safety that allows ideas to emerge. It helps employees open up and encourage each other. Open communication is key when working on a team and produces effective solutions in difficult group projects.

Without trust, a team crumbles and cannot succeed on assigned projects. Great teams build each other up and strengthen individual members to create a cohesive group. By working together, employees learn that wins and losses affect everyone on the team. Teamwork necessitates confidence in each other's distinct abilities.

4. Teaches Conflict Resolution Skills

Conflicts inevitably happen when you put together a group of unique people. Employees come from varied backgrounds and have different work styles and habits. While these unique viewpoints create the most successful work, they can also generate resentment that quickly turns into conflict.

When conflict arises in teamwork situations, employees are forced to resolve the conflicts themselves instead of turning to management. Learning conflict resolution firsthand is a skill that employees can use to become efficient managers down the road.

5. Promotes a Wider Sense of Ownership

Team projects encourage employees to feel proud of their contributions. Tackling obstacles and creating notable work together makes team members feel fulfilled. Working toward achieving company goals allows employees to feel connected to the company. This builds loyalty, leading to a higher level of job satisfaction among employees.

Teamwork is not just helpful for employees. It benefits the employer in the long run as well. Employees that connect directly with their workplace are more likely to stay with the company. While employees leaving their jobs often cite a lacking salary, another common complaint is that their contributions do not seem to matter. Teamwork allows people to engage with the company and add to the bigger picture.

6. Encourages Healthy Risk-Taking

An employee working on a project alone will probably not want to stick their neck out for an off-the-wall idea. If the project fails when working solo, that employee takes the full brunt of the blame. While you may not get full credit for a successful team project, working with other people spreads out the responsibility for a failed assignment.

Working as a team allows team members to take more risks, as they have the support of the entire group to fall back on in case of failure. Conversely, sharing success as a team is a bonding experience. Once a team succeeds together, their brainstorming sessions will produce revolutionary ideas without hesitation. In many cases, the riskiest idea turns out to be the best idea. Teamwork allows employees the freedom to think outside the box.

CHALLENGES OF TEAM/TEAMWORK

Teams may likely encounter some of the following problems:

1. Absence of team identity. Members may not feel mutually accountable to one another for the team's objectives. There may be a lack of commitment and effort, conflict between team goals and members' personal goals, or poor collaboration.

2. Difficulty making decisions. Team members may be rigidly adhering to their positions during decision making or making repeated arguments rather than introducing new information.

3. Poor communication. Team members may interrupt or talk over one another. There may be consistent silence from some members during meetings, allusions to problems but failure to formally address them, or false consensus (everyone nods in agreement without truly agreeing).

4. Inability to resolve conflicts. Conflicts can not be resolved when there are heightened tensions and team members make personal attacks or aggressive gestures.

5. Lack of participation. Team members fail to complete assignments. There may be poor attendance at team meetings or low energy during meetings.

6. Lack of creativity. The team is unable to generate fresh ideas and perspectives and doesn't turn unexpected events into opportunities.

7. Groupthink. The team is unwilling or unable to consider alternative ideas or approaches. There is a lack of critical thinking and debate over ideas. This often happens when the team overemphasizes team agreement and unity.

8. Ineffective leadership. Leaders can fail teams by not defining a compelling vision for the team, not delegating, or not representing multiple constituencies.

9. Lack of Growth mindset. Leaders often fail their teams when there's no long-term goals set to serve as a point they want to reach.

10. Lack of respect for individuals' ways of life. People from different backgrounds cannot behave the same, when the team fails to address issues resulting from morals and cultural decadence, the team will definitely collapse.

HOW TO MAINTAIN TEAMWORK

To maintain teamwork in every team, there's a need for each member of the team including the team leader to have the right attitude to work which includes:

1. Open communication to avoid conflicts: the leader and the team members should be open and transparent in their mode of communications at the workplace. There should be no room for sects within the team except on a special purpose; i.e if some people are selected for a particular task.

2. Effective coordination to avoid confusion and the overstepping of boundaries: the team's rules and regulations should be well stipulated to all its members. There should be some kinds of punishment for saboteurs just as there are rewards for high performance.

3. Workload Sharing: works within the team should be assigned to each member to allow efficient cooperation to perform the tasks in a timely manner and produce the required results.

4. Interdependence: trust should be built in the team to foster the feelings of team Spirit, high levels of interdependence, risk-taking, and performance.

5. Greetings and appraisal: method of rewards does not necessarily involve money or material things always. Reward could come in the form of gratitude or appraisal. For example, being thankful to the workers under you or giving a hand shake can go a long way in motivating the performer to keep to such a performance. It doesn't matter if it's a private or public firm. Once you are leading a group of people, you should form the habit of ownership.

CONCLUSION

For an effective teamwork system, there must be a high level of interdependence amongst the team members, a characteristic that stems from open communication and the increase of trust and risk-taking. Through interdependence come the group dynamics, which are the ways in which team members interact with each other. Sound dynamics makes the team members to be more satisfied and therefore working more efficiently together. But when there's a lack of sound dynamics, it leads to conflict, and it will disunite the team members. Due to this, an important characteristic of efficient teamwork is excellent conflict resolution that comes along with open communication. In order for efficient teamwork to exist, a team needs to have clear and attainable goals, through which team members can feel accomplished and motivated.

23

24

REFERENCES

A.O Andrew, 2009: *Elements of Special Education For Schools and Colleges*

Benjamin Samuel Bloom (1956): *Taxonomy of Educational Objectives: The Classification of Educational Goals, Volume 1*
https://en.wikipedia.org/wiki/Benjamin_Bloom

https://books.google.com/books/about/Taxonomy_of_Educational_Objectives.html?id=rJNqAAAAMAAJ

Quality Teams on ASQTV™
https://asq.org/quality-resources/teams

Wikipedia, Google

https://en.wikipedia.org/wiki/Teamwork

https://en.wikipedia.org/wiki/Team

https://en.wikipedia.org/wiki/Bloom%27s_taxonomy

About The Author

 **Hamza Suleiman**

Hamza Suleiman holds a Bachelor of Arts Education Degree from Kogi State University Anyigba, Nigeria. He is a Researcher, teacher and a virtual assistant who lives in Abuja, Nigeria. You can connect with him via LinkedIn: http://www.linkedin.com/in/hamza-suleiman,

Facebook: https://www.facebook.com/hamzaibn.suleiman, he also maintains a Facebook page (The Landslide Network).

www.ingramcontent.com/pod-product-compliance
Lightning Source LLC
Chambersburg PA
CBHW050328220526
45465CB00005B/2185